# Developing a Single Adult Ministry

## Bobbie Reed

**INTERNATIONAL CENTER FOR LEARNING**

A Subsidiary of G/L Publications, Glendale, California, U.S.A.

Published by International Center for Learning
G/L Publications Regal Books Division,
Glendale, California 91209
Printed in U.S.A.

ISBN 0-8307-0506-6

# Single Adults — Who Are They?

There they are! Every Sunday in every church in America. Filling the pews. Reading the bulletin. Singing the hymns. Listening to the sermon. Praying. Shaking hands with the pastor at the door. Going home...*alone*. The same way they came.

Who are we talking about? Single adults. The never married, divorced and widowed. The low profile people in your church. The gray people. The in-between people. The often ignored people. The incomplete people. That's how the rest of the church family usually views them.

Sad, tragic and true. The church often looks at this minority group in its midst and wishes it would go away. And many of them do.

But are they really a minority? National statistics indicate that there are over 47 million single adults in the United States today. That's an awesome number to ignore, but we often tend to ignore what we don't understand.

## The Never Married

We sometimes look at the never married as though they were not quite right or normal. Some of us try to match them up. Obviously if they would only get married and be like us, we would not have to understand them and attempt to meet their needs. Sometimes we just group all of the never married adults into one Sunday School class and call it "College-Career." But this doesn't always meet their needs.

## The Divorced

In many churches divorce has long been the unforgivable sin. Those who have terminated a marriage partnership by divorce might be asked to go elsewhere or risk the loss of membership and/or positions of leadership in their church. They are now among the permanently blemished. If they are allowed to stay around, the fear is that they could contaminate others. Little wonder their wounds, hurts, loneliness, guilt, frustration and fears go ignored. However, in many churches we are beginning to see a more forgiving and accepting attitude toward divorced persons.

## The Widowed

Suddenly single—but in this case by the death of a spouse. If above 50, they may be pitied and relegated to the church's golden age club. If under 50, they may be left to wander about in the coupled classes and groups with little understanding or care. Theirs is singlehood with honor; but it is a state often as lonely, misunderstood and uncared for as the never married and divorced.

Three distinct groups of people with two common distinctions—unmarried and largely ignored by the church.[1]

This booklet is designed to present the challenge and some suggestions for beginning an effective ministry to the adults in your church who may have often wished that they were not single.

# Why Single Out Singles?

Beautiful, petite Kerrie reaching out to shake the pastor's hand Sunday morning, recoiled as he greeted her, "Where's that husband of yours this morning?"

"Where indeed!" she thought, bursting into tears. The pain of his recent desertion was still too near the surface for her to take even the most innocent comments lightly. "Overreacting about Phil's departure seems to be a way of life these days," she beat herself mentally. "And I came to church for help!" she thought ruefully.

But is she getting help? Frequently pastors and Christian education directors ask us "Why do we need to single out singles? We can just incorporate them into the regular adult Bible study classes." Some singles may attend these Bible classes. But many more do not. We single out singles so that we can better minister to their unique needs.

Single and married adults are alike in many ways. In each situation a person may have the similar responsibilities of maintaining a home, upholding a job, balancing a budget, juggling a schedule, and bringing up children. But in many areas the single person has special needs—

particularly those persons who have recently become divorced or widowed.

Problems faced by a person newly divorced or widowed may range from reconstructing one's identity to solving a financial crisis. Single parenting has unique problems no matter which parent has custody. The emotional shock of adjusting to a radically different life-style can have a tremendous effect on a person—positive or negative.

Yes, the needs are many, but the challenges are unlimited! What a fertile field for God to plant. What an opportunity for us to watch these people grow as God heals their hurts and rebuilds their lives. Since most singles are in the midst of change and growth in their own lives, they will respond eagerly to the fellowship and direction of people-caring churches.

## What to Expect When Singling Out Singles

Leaders of successful single adult ministries have shared their experiences with us. Here are some of the things to expect of a single adult class.

***Singles will come for different reasons.*** Single adults come to church and Bible study for different reasons. The following is a list of some of them.

- to grow spiritually (sometimes a low priority reason).
- to satisfy a longing for fellowship and contact with other single adults.
- to receive comfort, understanding and acceptance.
- to sustain the "habit" of going to church.
- to ease the conscience that says they "should" go to church.
- to take their children.
- to get the social activity calendar or announcements.

- to meet a potential marriage partner.
- to make a last effort at getting their lives back together.
- to find a reason to live.
- to serve Christ through the church!

Whatever the reason they come at first, be ready. Provide an atmosphere which accepts them as they are and an uplifting program which meets them at their level of need.

**Singles stay for different reasons.** Singles will flow in and out of a class or singles' group. If you checked your membership roles every six months, an average of about half of the members would be new.

Basically, singles will remain in a Sunday School class or Bible study group as long as the group continues to meet their needs. As in any group, a person who is searching for the "meat of the Word" will probably not linger if the sessions serve only "milk." But many singles are also coming for companionship—they want to talk to somebody. Often they live alone without the benefit of a live-in companion with whom to talk over their daily ups and downs. It is doubtful that singles will remain in a class which stifles discussion or prohibits the sharing of experiences.

Your singles will be at different stages of personal and spiritual growth. Never marrieds may be dealing with social pressures that they "should" marry. The recently divorced or widowed often tend to spend a lot of time focusing on their divorce or bereavement. They need many opportunities to share and to receive love and acceptance.

It would be a mistake to begin a singles' ministry without being aware of and taking into consideration these many needs and problems of singles. But it would be an even greater mistake to try and make every Bible study session address each level of need! Instead, plan to provide for needs at different levels during different activities—over a weekly, monthly, or yearly schedule.

**People will be prejudiced.** Prejudices will be found among singles and marrieds. Many never marrieds will not attend family-oriented Bible studies or activities planned by the couples' classes. Many divorced and widowed find it painful to be in classes and activities where others are so obviously "coupled."

Church members are sometimes suspicious and misunderstanding of singles and therefore stand aloof. The lack of understanding and failure to communicate openly have created barriers. Some married folk may find the single adult life attractive and therefore threatening to their own life-style. A husband or wife may feel that exposure to single life may cause their spouse to desire more freedom than they have in marriage.

***Some singles will decide to marry.*** Be aware that when you have a singles' ministry, there will probably be singles who decide to marry. The church has traditionally rejoiced and celebrated this decision for single adults who have either never been married before, or are widowed. But the biblical sanction of remarriage after divorce is still a theologically debatable issue.

The pastor and leaders in a single adult ministry should openly discuss how they will handle this situation should it arise. They should pray together, study the Scriptures which apply, and consult reliable resources as they seek the guidance of the Holy Spirit in this area.

## What Are the Benefits of Singling Out Singles?

The benefits of planning for a separate single adult ministry include:
- Special needs will be addressed, therefore singles will be assisted in coping with their own individual problems.
- Singles will be given time and space to stretch and grow at their own pace.
- Companionship will be provided by other singles who can relate

at an experience level and offer genuine understanding and acceptance.

■ Singles who are hurting can begin to heal as they reach out to share with and to help each other.

## Singles and the Body of Christ

The Christian education committee was about to conclude its monthly meeting when Lisa Rogers, the Children's Division Coordinator, spoke up. "I know this subject isn't on our agenda, but we at least need to start thinking about a couple to replace Skip and Nancy Faulkner, our Junior Department leaders. Skip is being transferred to the West Coast this summer. Anybody have any ideas?"

The four other committee members sat thoughtfully for a minute. "How about the Lawrences?" someone offered.

"I've talked to them before about working with us," Lisa reported, "but they don't want to commit themselves to a weekly responsibility."

Several other couples were suggested, but each was discounted for one reason or another.

"Say!" the general superintendent exclaimed as an idea burst upon him. "Chuck Polaski from the singles' group has been asking me about working with juniors. Maybe he and another one of our singles could work together as a team in the Junior Department."

"Great idea," Lisa chirped. "I'll ask Chuck and some of the others. I guess I've overlooked the potential that we have in that active singles' group."

Singles need to be integrated into the ministry of the Body of Christ, just as does any other member. Providing a separate ministry to singles does not mean that they should be totally separated from the Body of the church at all times. They should be invited to participate at various levels, for example service projects, Christian education leadership training and fellowship activities. One single paraphrased Ephesians 4:11,12 to communicate this same message. "And He gave some as youth, some as married, some as senior citizens, some as children—and some as singles—for the equipping of the saints for the work of service to the building up of the Body of Christ."[2]

As you minister to your single adults both as a special need group and as an integral part of the Body of Christ, your church will grow. You will be utilizing the talents in your church and there will be an increased unity throughout the congregation as you all work together for His glory.

# Starting the Single Adult Ministry

In a recent conversation, the pastor of a middle-sized congregation stated that he was not aware of any single adults in his church. He seemed to feel that since no one had come to him personally, and volunteered the information that they were single, he did not need to consider a specialized ministry to singles. He was encouraged to insert a card in the bulletin the following Sunday and ask all never marrieds, divorced and widowed to fill in the information required to evaluate the need for a singles' ministry.

The surprising yield was 43 responses! He couldn't believe it. The singles were there just waiting to be identified.

## Find Out Who Your Singles Are

One of the quickest and easiest ways to identify your singles is to insert a card in the church bulletin requesting name, address, telephone number, occupation, single status (never married, divorced, widowed) and age range (18–25, 25–35, etc.).

## Find Out What the Needs Are

After you have tabulated the survey of singles in your church, invite those who filled out cards to a special planning meeting. Do this even if only one or two people responded. You may wish to meet informally in the pastor's home, or the home of a person who is a potential leader for a singles' ministry in your church.

At the planning meeting, remember that your agenda includes identifying the interests and needs of your single adults. Don't assume what the needs are—ask! Are most of your singles coming to church in search of Christian acceptance, comfort, caring relationships, fellowship with believers, or spiritual growth? Do they want help with the special challenges of being single? Find out.

Start your meeting by explaining that your church wants to be responsive to all of its members, and to provide a ministry to all who visit the services or programs. Ask those who attend the meeting to brainstorm three lists:

1. Ways our church effectively ministers to singles (things not to change).

2. Ways our church partially ministers to singles (things to do more of).

3. Ways our church does not minister to singles (things to start doing).

After the group has brainstormed these lists, take time to discuss the ideas expressed. A potential program will take shape as these interests and ideas are articulated.

## Plan Your Ministry

After you have discussed ideas for a program, making plans for your ministry is the next step. This may be an agenda item for the first planning meeting, a task reserved for a second meeting of interested singles, or a task for the pastor and a couple of representatives from the planning meeting. Some of your plans will be short-range—things you can begin right away. Other plans will be long-range—things you will work toward. Select two or three areas which have the highest priority, discuss these, and plan how you will begin. Here are a few examples.

# Some Ingredients to Consider

## A Bible Study for Singles

Adults never outgrow the need for Bible study. So your singles should be in a weekly Bible study class. In discussing your plan, you will want to consider these questions:

Do you want to create a separate Sunday School class for singles?

Is the present adult Bible study curriculum in your church applicable to the needs of single adults?

Should you begin a special Bible study covering topics of concern to singles?

As you plan, remember that you can start a Bible study with as few as three or four singles who are enthusiastic about learning from God's Word together. One of the most successful singles' classes (in terms of sharing, growing spiritually, caring for the needs of *each* member, and fellowship) I've visited had only eight members!

If you are not ready to begin a singles' class in your church, you might encourage your single adults to attend some functions for singles at a larger church in your area (when those functions do not conflict with your own church activities). Or, if your community does not have a large church providing activities, fellowship or Bible studies for singles, then several small churches might co-sponsor a singles' ministry. Or, you may decide to work on another plan first ...like outreach!

***The Bible Study Session.*** When you begin a Bible study session, start with coffee and donuts to set a warm, comfortable atmosphere. Encourage people to get acquainted with each other, and once you get going, be sure to introduce visitors each week, and help them feel included. One way to help people get better acquainted and feel comfortable is to plan a simple fellowship activity for the first few minutes of each Bible study session.

As you move into the Bible study, remember to involve your adults in the learning process. Involve them in exploring God's Word and in discovering how the biblical truths apply to their own lives. Encourage your singles to make positive life changes based on the principles they discover in God's Word.

Assistance in understanding how adults learn, planning effective sessions, and using effective Bible learning methods is found in the ICL handbook, *Creative Bible Learning for Adults* by Monroe Marlowe and Bobbie Reed (Regal, 1977).

***Organizing the Class.*** Some people shy away from organization in any form because of past experiences where organization was overemphasized. But operating without any organization results in confusion and ineffectiveness.

Every singles' group requires just enough organization to prevent confusion. The amount of organization you will want will depend on the size and scope of your own individual group. The purpose of organizing your group is to limit the responsibility assigned to one person or committee for maximum effectiveness. As your program changes, your organization will need to be altered accordingly.

Analyze your group to determine how many leaders you will need. The most significant determinant is group size. How many regular members do you have? Do you have five to fifteen singles? You may only want one or two leaders at first. Do you have fifty or more singles? You may want several leaders right away.

The basic leadership positions, or officers, are: class leader (who may be called president), teacher, secretary, unit leaders, social chairperson, and possibly a treasurer. This team directs and coordinates the group functions in all areas including: membership, outreach, fellowship, family life, publicity, music, spiritual life, and group caring.

As your group grows, you may form committees for each of these major functions and involve more of your members in planning and conducting your activities. Committees, of course, do not function autonomously, but rather require guidance from your group leaders. Committees have the advantage of getting several people involved in planning and implementing the mission of your group. The more people you involve, the greater is your potential for creativity. Also, people who are actively involved tend to maintain enthusiasm for and interest in a singles' group.

In order to provide the opportunity for effective learning, the size of any adult class should be limited to 30–40. When your group reaches this number, you have the opportunity to refine your ministry by dividing into two classes. Many large singles' groups are successfully divided according to age level.

Under the direction of effective leaders, your program will begin to meet the wants and needs of your singles. The word will spread, and your group will grow and grow and grow! Soon you may have your own singles' department with several classes. You may decide you need a full-time minister to single adults on your church staff. He will supervise all other leaders within the group, and be able to assist in more in-depth ministries as counseling, workshops and staff training.

More information for organization, including job descriptions for class leaders, is found in *Creative Bible Learning for Adults.*

***Recruiting Leaders.*** One of the most frequently asked questions is "Where do I find leaders for singles' groups?" Here are some ideas.

First, ask God for guidance. He has given each person talents and gifts. Who knows best which people possess the appropriate gifts to fill your leadership vacancies? He does!

Then begin looking for people who have a heart for ministry. Also try to find people who have demonstrated their gifts in leadership and administration. Get to know your singles as personally as possible. Discover their individual interests, strengths, and gifts. Learn which singles are ready to serve.

Next, know the specific leadership positions you want to fill and the special requirements of each. Don't be guilty of misrepresenting a position because of ignorance. Keep informed of your church's policies and procedures for selecting and appointing official leaders.

Finally, approach people with a positive attitude. Recruiting leaders is exciting! You're offering an opportunity to exercise individual gifts! Don't try to get leaders by making people feel guilty if they say no. Don't just "take turns" serving as leaders. Be positive and find the best leaders for your class.

***Choosing Classroom Space.*** The physical setting for your single adult Bible study is critical. If you put your singles into any leftover space you can find, your group will not feel very important to the church. You will want the classroom to be as attractive, roomy and as comfortable as possible to set an atmosphere where fellowship and learning can occur. The arrangement of the equipment within the room will also have an important effect on creating an atmosphere of warmth and acceptance.

One way is to arrange the chairs in a circle to promote personal interaction. This allows each adult to face another as well as to have his neighbor partially face him.

The desired atmosphere of warmth and acceptance can be enhanced even more by breaking the large group into smaller units for discussion and exchange of ideas. Small groups promote participation, self-perception, and knowledge of others in the group.

There are several places you can hold your singles' class. A classroom in the *church* is a convenient and familiar setting to most people. A *home* belonging to one of the members has the advantage of being warm, friendly, and informal. The size of your group may determine the convenience of using a home.

Holding a Bible study in the *recreation room* of a group member's apartment building is a great outreach technique. People who might never attend a church service or go to a group meeting in a church may come to a gathering in their own building. Attendance may be motivated by curiosity, loneliness, or genuine interest. What counts is that people come!

Some restaurants, coffee shops and banks allow groups to use one of their *conference rooms* free of charge or for a small fee. Again, a neutral location will attract people who may not otherwise attend an in-church meeting. Also, two or more small churches might sponsor the Bible study to be held in a public building. This provides a way for singles from several churches to get together and share as they study God's Word.

## Reaching Unchurched Singles

A second plan you may wish to concentrate on is reaching the unchurched singles in your community. Consider these questions as you plan.

How many of the single adult members of your church attend regularly? Why do some come and others do not?

How many widowed, divorced or single parents live in your community? (Census information is available through your local library.)

How many single parents of the children in your Sunday School attend your church?

What alternatives to attending your church are offered to singles in your area (*e.g.* clubs, programs at other churches, etc.)? Contact these associations and identify what things they are doing which are successful in bringing in the singles. They may have some good ideas you will want to copy.

Where are the singles in your immediate community (single apartment buildings, military bases, colleges, etc.)?

How can you determine the potential of your program (door-to-door campaigns, mailed questionnaires, or "would-you-be-interested" meetings)?

When you have assessed the single adults you wish to reach, and identified a few ways to get started, then get started!

## Providing Fellowship for Singles

"What are your hobbies? What do you do to relax?" the doctor asked as he reviewed Brad's chart.

"Hobbies?" Brad laughed bitterly. "You've got to be kidding! I'm new in town and just going through a divorce. What would I do for fun?"

What do your singles do when they feel the need for recreation, relaxation, entertainment and fun? Your church can do a great service to the singles in its membership by providing opportunities for meeting the social needs of the unmarrieds.

Does the calendar of events for your single adults look a little bare? It doesn't have to be! With a little creativity and imagination, your calendar can include activities and opportunities for single adults of all ages and interests.

Involve your singles in planning monthly events. Announce a planning meeting and invite anyone who is interested to attend. At the meeting, brainstorm activities, discuss the possibilities and finalize the calendar.

Here are some guidelines you may wish to follow:

1. Plan each month's activities at least a month ahead of time. (When planning, check the church calendar. You will want to avoid conflicts with other functions planned for church members.)

2. Duplicate the monthly calendars and distribute to members and visitors.

3. Include directions to and telephone numbers of homes and locations where activities will be held.

4. Plan a variety of activities such as: weekly Bible study (Sunday mornings or weekday evenings); opportunities for service (volunteer work on church projects, visits to nursing homes or hospitals); social activities (parties, get-togethers, sports, camping); talk-it-overs (small group-guided discussions).

5. Keep individual and group costs in mind. Balance your more expensive activities (ski weekends or camp-outs) with events which cost little or nothing (game night at someone's home with everybody bringing homemade snacks).

6. Plan some activities "for adults only" as well as activities which will include children of the group members.

7. You may wish to arrange child care during some of your activities. This may be paid for from the group treasury, by individual parents using the service, or by collecting donations at the activity.

8. Realize that not all of your singles will come to all of your activities. Provide for a variety of interests.

9. Ideally, you will want to plan one activity per week besides Sunday morning. They don't all need to be elaborate—just an opportunity for singles to get together.

10. Don't get into a rut! Plan different activities each month. A list of activities is provided to give you some ideas:

Amusement park, archery, art shows (professional or do your own), art gallery visit, baking party for the holidays, bus ride, bowling, boating, bird-watching, baseball, bicycling, breakfast out, barbecue, circus, camping, car races, community recreation programs and classes, drives (to see lights at holidays or flowers in bloom), fishing, game night (table games at someone's home), holiday theme parties, hiking, hunting, horseback riding, museum visit, music concert, out for dinner, picnics (beach, park, backyard), plays, play tourist in your own city, picture taking, progressive dinners, potluck dinners, skating (ice or roller), swimming, state or county fairs, sailing, sewing get together, softball, sledding, snowshoeing, skiing, tobogganing, target shooting, taffy pull, volleyball, visiting another singles' group, water-skiing, walking.

## Caring for Your Singles

A newly divorced young man related his experience to us. "One Sunday I went to church out of loneliness and desperation. The minister announced a Bible study for singles, and I immediately planned to attend. When the night arrived, I kept coming up with reasons for not going. What if they're all as depressed as I am? What if they don't really approve of a divorced person? What if they're all 'super Christians'? I haven't been to church in quite awhile.

"Somehow in spite of my arguments, I nervously drove to the church meeting. The smell of hot coffee reached me in the parking lot, and I heard people talking and laughing. As I entered the large room, I saw people standing in groups eating donuts, drinking coffee and it seemed to me then that EVERY ONE OF THEM WAS SMILING! A man approached me, a big grin on his face, his hand extended, and said, 'Since you're not wearing one of our badges, I'll assume you're a visitor. Welcome, my name is Bill.'

"He walked me to a table where I signed in and received a name tag. He handed me an activity calendar, then introduced me to several of the people in the room. When he excused himself, I had an opportunity to look around again. The room was large and chairs were arranged in small circles around the room. The atmosphere was open and roomy. The people were warm and friendly. By the time we began our small group discussions, I felt as though I really belonged!"

How would a visitor rate the caring level of your Sunday School? How would a member describe the caring level?

We are all drawn together by relationships and a need for belonging and being close. Most adults find satisfaction for this need in marriage or other close relationships. But single adults often must step outside their bachelor's apartment to find close, caring relationships. You must plan for caring! It doesn't just happen. Oh, sure, some people will be loved. Some people will love others. That's their personality. But, what about the others? If there are no caring relationships, there is a void. That void will be felt most by those who don't love or accept love easily.

*Caring Units.* We must work toward warmth and acceptance for everyone in our singles' program. One way to plan for caring is to appoint a caring coordinator for the singles' class. This leader cares for members, keeps in regular, close contact with all members by phone calls, visits and cards as needed. He encourages members to participate in Sunday School, worship services, other church activities, socials and special projects. He visits the sick and absent members, and communicates needs to the class teacher.

When your singles' group has grown to 30 or 40 members, you may consider dividing the group into several caring units with caring coordinators for each unit. This smaller grouping within the class, or no more than six persons under the leadership of a caring coordinator, provides fellowship, caring and sharing, and intimate relationships for growing Christians.

Unit members warmly welcome new members by sitting with them in worship services, going out with them to coffee after church, and including them in unit activities. They reach new prospects by inviting them to unit activities, and visiting referrals and prospects. They share with and care for each other.

As a result of caring units, people have opportunities to use their gifts; people are cared for individually and personally; people are not "lost in the crowd" of a large class; and people are more active in their small groups than they would be in one large class.

For more details on organizing and facilitating caring units, see the ICL booklet *The Adult Class: Caring for Each Other*, by Neal McBride (Regal, 1977).

***SOS (Serving Other Singles).*** Carol arrived at the singles' session with red, puffy eyes. "What's the matter?" asked a concerned friend. And Carol, no longer able to hold her tears back, blurted out, "I just don't know what I'm going to do. My landlord gave me three days to come up with my rent money or I'll be evicted. The child support check still hasn't come. I don't have the money. I keep thinking of the kids, and I just don't know what we're going to do."

While Carol was desperately trying to regain her composure, her friend acted quickly. Within a few minutes Carol was given a check from the class emergency fund.

As the initials SOS imply, <u>Serving Other Singles</u> is an emergency rescue ministry of the singles' class. It is a practical burden-bearing provision for any in the group who have an emergency need.

Serving other singles with <u>financial assistance is not always</u> an <u>emergency situation</u>. One group which plans two or three major functions a year which may cost $30–$50 a person (or family) has a scholarship fund. The functions include <u>retreats</u>, <u>weekend camp-outs</u>, or <u>Christian seminars</u>. The fund is replenished by donations, special offerings, garage sales, and sometimes by singles who later can afford to and do "repay" the fund.

Serving each other doesn't always involve money. One group has a bulletin board where members "advertise" needs and opportunities. "Help! I'm moving next Wednesday and could use some help!" one girl wrote. Job openings are shared with group members through this method. One large singles' class published a "Service Directory" in which members advertised their professional services (real estate, income tax preparations, housekeeping, child care, photography). Group members were encouraged to purchase services from other members whenever possible.

Another group has a good idea. One Saturday each month they hold "help-each-other-work-day." The guys go to the gals' homes to do heavy-duty work or odd repair jobs. These might include car tune-ups, minor carpenter or plumbing, tree trimming, major yard clean up, or housepainting. The women reciprocate by helping the guys with mending, sewing, interior decorating, and serving home cooked "favorite" meals. So, in helping each other, the singles grow and help themselves.

***Single Parent Assistance.*** A critical problem with the single parent is the change in parent-child relationships after the divorce or death of a spouse. One parent now has sole custody or major responsibility for rearing the children. The child now has only one parent (either mom or dad) around most of the time to provide discipline, love and role models. And the non-custodial parent in a divorce situation has lost the day-to-day relationship he may have had with his children.

One way to help alleviate all three of these needs is a type of Big Brother or Big Sister program in your church. A Christian man (married or single) prayerfully signs up to spend some of his time with a child who has no father in the home. Or, a Christian woman (married or single) prayerfully commits part of her time to a child without a mother at home.

The time they spend together may involve special activities such as swimming, hiking, playing tennis, bowling; or may be spent on non-special, everyday activities like cooking, cleaning the garage, grocery shopping, washing the car or sewing. The emphasis should not be on indulging the child, but on caring for the child and sharing with him in a way to round out his life activities.

This program allows other Christians to share the emotional burden of child rearing with the single parent. It gives the child a balance of mother-father image relationships. Furthermore, it also may provide healing for the wounds of a Big Brother or Sister who has lost a close relationship with his own children.

This program is not intended to solve all of the problems of single parenting. But it is one way to help care for one another.

Another way to provide assistance to single parents is to arrange for child care during class time and whenever there are special functions. Child care may be paid for by the class, by parents using the "service" or may be a co-op arrangement where parents trade off the responsibility of "baby-sitting" for the other parents.

*Counseling.* You show that you care for someone when you listen to him. We all want to be listened to when we have something to say! We talk when we are riding the crest of the wave of success. We talk when we are lonely. We need to talk when grieving the death of a spouse or when agonizing through a divorce.

Sometimes we just need a person to listen and not respond. Sometimes we need an empathetic shoulder to cry on. Other times we are seeking specific guidance and counsel. You may want to provide training in peer counseling for some of the leaders of your singles' group. They will learn to be sensitive to the needs of the group members and be able to know when to refer people with serious problems for professional help.

Physical problems must be referred to a medical doctor. Legal problems must be handled by an attorney. Career or educational problems belong to Christian educators. Psychological problems can be resolved with help from a psychiatrist or psychologist. Serious spiritual problems may be referred to the pastor or other spiritual leaders in your church.

Locate resources in your church and community. Make a list of these leaders with their phone numbers and keep it handy.

In addition to the above mentioned caring activities, you may wish to include a 24-hour telephone dial-help line, a mini-library with books of special interest to singles, or a newsletter specifically for your singles.

You will have other ideas which will foster caring relationships, involvement and helping. Whatever methods you choose, you will find that in caring for your singles, you begin to build a sense of community in the Body of Christ.

## Providing a Forum for Sharing

Weekly small group discussions can contribute more to group closeness than any one other aspect of the singles' ministry. These discussions are most effective if scheduled for a weeknight (not Fridays, that's date night for many singles) and if called something like "Talk-It-Over" or "Care and Share."

All discussions should be started with introductions of each member of the group. The discussions can be guided by the group leaders using a ditto sheet of prepared topics relevant to the group. The topics are designed to encourage self-awareness and sharing.

Topics must be very carefully chosen too that they will be of interest to and deal with the problems of singles. Yet, they must be positive and promote emotional and spiritual growth. Some topics are just naturally more interesting than others and intriguing titles will help promote attendance. Consider these: God's principles for building relationships, single parenting, developing a positive self-image, growing through divorce or widowhood, forgiveness, starting over, Christian growth, the Christian single and sex, time and budget management, and subjects such as loneliness and depression.

Representatives from the singles' group should be involved in the selection of discussion topics. Bible verses relating to the discussion topic should be listed on the discussion guide sheets which are distributed to all group leaders before the sessions.

Large groups should be divided into smaller groups, each with a leader, to promote greater involvement in the discussion. Every group uses the same questions, giving a spirit of oneness in the room. This also encourages cross-group or one-to-one discussions after the meetings.

Some flexibility is allowed so that the well-trained group leader who is in tune to the needs of his group may concentrate more on one aspect of the planned discussion than another in order to meet those needs. At the end of the discussion, the session is closed in prayer by the leader or a group member.

## Publicize Your Program

When you are ready to start, you should enthusiastically publicize your program. Yours may be the best program going for singles in the community. But if you don't "spread the word" it may take a long time to get off the ground.

Brainstorm as many publicity ideas as possible before you select those you will use. Here's a list to get you started: announcements in Sunday School, worship services and other church-related activities; colorful flyers (use door-to-door, public bulletin boards, mailouts, send home with Sunday School children, pass out to people as they leave supermarkets, put on windshields of parked cars); posters (at colleges, sporting goods stores, beauty salons, barbershops, local markets); door-to-door visitation; advertisements in newspapers; bring-a-friend activities; articles in local newspapers; and TV or radio community scene spots.

Any advertising agent will tell you that the most effective publicity is the personal testimonial of a satisfied customer. So it will be for your singles' ministry once it gets rolling. When the singles of your church find that their spiritual, social and emotional needs are being met by the singles' program, they will pass the word to their friends and your group will grow.

So take advantage of both avenues of publicity. Use appropriate "mass media" advertising to keep your program in the public eye. But more importantly, concentrate on meeting needs in your singles' group and you will be amazed at how the news will get around about the singles' ministry in your church.

## Things to Remember



Now that you're all excited and ready to start...take a few minutes to count the cost of such a program and to think on these things:

***Approach the Task Seriously.*** Do not start your program on the spur of the moment, as a whim. Lay a foundation of careful thought and prayer. Sit down and count the cost of time and effort to be sure you will be able to maintain the program. (See Luke 14:28-30.)

***View Problem-Solving Realistically.*** Do not feel that through your program you will able to solve problems for single members in your church or community. It can't. People have to solve their own problems with God's help. However, your singles' ministry can provide the framework and the setting for them to begin to solve their own problems. Remember to care but to remain objective. You will see some singles succeed. You will also see some fail. So do not be discouraged. Turn your program over to God and let Him work through it.

***Cling to Your Goal Tenaciously.*** Remember that your goal is to encourage growth toward self-reliance in your singles. As time for adjustment is allowed (the length will vary from individual to individual) you will see this growth. As leadership ability and willingness to assume responsibility arise from within the group, take advantage of it! Use singles to run the program, as soon as possible.

***Start, but Start Slowly.*** A new singles' ministry grows by trial and error and by steps. Don't try to land on the top step in the first jump. Ask for help and ideas. Find out what other churches are doing. Go visit their programs. Talk to leaders of singles' groups. Identify pitfalls and problems to avoid. Plan together. If you only have a small church with a handful of singles, join with several other churches. Form an inter-church group that can meet and grow together and still let people function in their own church on other levels.

The fact that you don't have any single adults who attend your church regularly does not mean that you do not need a ministry to the singles. It only means that you are not presently meeting the need of single adults in your church or community.

Do something today! Get something started! Assure the singles in your church and community that "flying solo" is just as much a gift from God, and opportunity for ministry, as "flying tandem."

---

## Footnotes

1. Jim Smoke, "Single on Sunday," *Theology News and Notes* (Fuller Theological Seminary, March 1976), p. 2.
2. Janet Fix, "We Need a Family," *Christian Life* (October 1976), p. 54.

# Bibliography


Ahlem, Lloyd. *Do I Have to be Me?* Glendale, CA: Regal Books, 1973.

Andrews, Gini. *Your Half of the Apple.* Grand Rapids, MI: Zondervan Publishing House, 1972.

Becker, Russell J. *When Marriage Ends.* Philadelphia, PA: Fortress Press, 1971.

Bel Geddes, Joan. *How to Parent Alone; A Guide for Single Parents.* New York, NY: Seabury Press, 1974.

Bohannan, Paul, ed. *Divorce and After.* Garden City, NY: Doubleday and Co., 1971.

Bontrager, Frances. *The Church and the Single Person.* Scottsdale, PA: Herald Press, 1969.

Champagne, Manan. *Facing Life Alone.* Hauppauge, NY: Universal Publishing and Distributing Corp., 1969.

Decker, Beatrice and Kooiman, Gladys. *After the Flowers Have Gone.* Grand Rapids, MI: Zondervan Publishing House, 1973.

Edwards, Marie, and Hoover, Eleanor. *The Challenge of Being Single.* New York, NY: J.P. Tarcher, Inc., 1974.

Epstein, Joseph. *Divorced in America: An Anatomy of Loneliness.* New York, NY: E.P. Dutton and Co., 1974.

Evening, Margaret. *Who Walk Alone.* Downers Grove, IL: Inter-Varsity Press, 1974.

Fisher, Esther O. *Divorce: The New Freedom.* Scranton, PA: Harper and Row, 1972.

Gardner, Richard. *The Boys and Girls Book About Divorce.* New York: Aronson, Jason, Inc., 1971.

Guder, Eileen L. *We're Never Alone.* Grand Rapids, MI: Zondervan Publishing House, 1965.

Hardisty, Margaret. *Forever My Love.* Irvine, CA: Harvest House, 1975.

Hope, Karol, and Young, Nancy. *Momma Handbook: The Source Book for Single Mothers.* New York, NY: Time Change Press, 1976.

Hosier, Helen K. *The Other Side of Divorce.* New York, NY: Hawthorn Books, 1975.

Hudson, R. Lofton. *Til Divorce Do Us Part.* Nashville: Thomas Nelson, Inc., 1974.

Jepson, Sarah. *For the Love of Singles.* Carol Stream, IL: Creation House, 1970.

Krantzler, Mel. *Creative Divorce: A New Opportunity for Personal Growth.* Philadelphia, PA: M. Evans and Co., 1973.

Maddox, Brenda. *The Half-Parent.* New York, NY: New American Library, 1976.

McGinnis, Marilyn. *Single.* Old Tappan, NJ: Fleming H. Revell, Co., 1976.

Moore, Allen J. *The Young Adult Generation.* New York, NY: Abingdon Press, 1971.

Morse, Theresa A. *Life Is for Living.* Garden City, NY: Doubleday, 1973.

Payne, Dorothy. *Women Without Men.* Philadelphia, PA: United Church Press, 1969.

Peppler, Alice S. *Divorced and Christian.* St. Louis, MO: Concordia Publishing House, 1974.

Roosevelt, Ruth, and Lofas, Jeanette. *Living in Step.* New York: NY: Stein and Day, 1976.

Sands, Audrey L. *Single and Satisfied.* Wheaton, IL: Tyndale House, 1971.

Schuller, Robert H. *You Can Become the Person You Want to Be.* New York: Hawthorn Books, 1976.

Sheehy, Gail. *Passages: Predictable Crises of Adult Life.* New York, NY: E.P. Dutton and Co., 1976.

Small, Dwight H. *The Right to Remarry.* Old Tappan, NJ: Fleming H. Revell, Co., 1975.

Smoke, Jim. *Growing Through Divorce.* Irvine, CA: Harvest House, 1976.

Start, Clarissa. *When You're a Widow.* St. Louis, MO: Concordia Publishing House, 1973.

Stewart, Suzanne. *Divorced...I Wouldn't Have Given a Nickel for Your Chances!* Grand Rapids, MI: Zondervan Publishing House, 1974.

Weiss, Robert S., ed. *Loneliness.* Cambridge, MA: M.I.T. Press, 1973.

Weiss, Robert S. *Marital Separation.* New York, NY: Basic Books, 1975.

*Solo,* a magazine specifically for singles, is published bimonthly by the Positive Christian Singles of Garden Grove Community Church, 12141 Lewis Street, Garden Grove, CA 92640.




*The publishers do not necessarily endorse the entire contents of all publications referred to in this booklet.*